Mianus Village

ALSO BY JACK T. SCULLY

SHORT STORIES

"Louie," *The Gleaner*, Burlington, VT

"Until Labor Day," *The Vermont Cynic*, Burlington, VT

"A Child's Christmas in Connecticut," *Greenwich Stories and Opinions*, Facebook Page: https://www.facebook.com/groups/grstories

NOVELS

Eyewitness, Kindle and Nook e-books, Amazon and Barnes & Noble, May 20, 2011

Summer of '65, manuscript

WEBSITE & FACEBOOK PAGE

"Beyond Gridlock and Greed" with J. Chris Davala: https://medium. com and https://www.facebook.com/BeyondGridlockandGreed

Mianus Village

Poems by

Jack T. Scully

Antrim House

Bloomfield, Connecticut

Library of Congress Control Number: 2021909071

ISBN: 978-1-943826-84-1

First Edition, 2021

Printed & bound by Ingram Content Group

Book design by Rennie McQuilkin

Front cover photograph by Inga Skuratovsky

Author photograph by Beltrami & Co. Photography

Antrim House
860.217.0023
AntrimHouseBooks@gmail.com
www.AntrimHouseBooks.com
400 Seabury Dr., #5196, Bloomfield, CT 06002

For my mother
Mary Barnes Scully
(1918-1968)

ACKNOWLEDGMENTS

Grateful acknowledgment to the editors of the publications in which the following poems first appeared, at times in earlier versions:

"Coming Home," *The Burlington Review*, Burlington, VT

"Uncle Johnnie in the Living Room," and "How I Cured Dante of Dares" (as "How Dante Was Cured of Doing Dangerous Things"), *The Vermont Cynic*, Burlington, VT

"Why Father MacNamara Went to Caribou," *The Gleaner*, Burlington, VT and *Tinderbox*, Mt Pleasant, SC

"When Krissy Lee Stood Up" and "Widow Hudson," *Tinderbox,* Mt. Pleasant, SC

"The Day the Music Died," "The Natural," "Tod's Point," and "Frog Legs," *Greenwich CT Stories and Opinions,* Facebook Page, https://www.facebook.com/StoriesandOpinions

The following special thanks. To my wife and partner, Wendy Chapman Scully, for her constant love and encouragement in our journey through life. To my children, Kerry and Michael, whose loving natures, humility, and accomplishments have always made us proud. To my brother, Dennis, who knows well the light and shade of these *Mianus Village* poems. And to my creative writing professors, David Huddle, John Engels, and Alan Broughton, who gave me the tools and motivation to write colloquial poems celebrating life in simple, clear, and imaginative terms.

TABLE OF CONTENTS

Deep in our subconscious... lie all our memories...
Forgotten debris of forgotten years
Waiting to be recalled...
Waiting for some small, intimate reminder...
An echo from the past...

– Noel Coward, *Nothing Is Lost*

Mianus Village

Entries in a Family Bible

In 1847 at age 18,
my great-great-grandfather,
Patrick Doran,
scared and alone,
landed in Manhattan
from Ireland
with 52 pence in his pocket—
enough to chug 28 miles
up the tracks
to Greenwich, Connecticut
but no farther.
He jumped off
an open carriage car,
side-stepped piles of dung
on Railroad Avenue
and spotted a *Help Wanted* sign
at a livery stable.
Patrick paused in the barn door
and rubbed his soot-smudged cheeks
before bowing to the owner, Darius Mead,
all the time
worried his brogue,
thick as spud stew,
would evoke a cry of rebuke
before he could say
he knew how to shoe horses
and wasn't too proud
to muck out stalls.
He had no education,
he said, but he knew ponies
and they liked him. Sensing
the sweetness of the boy's nature,

Mr. Mead held out
a calloused hand
and hired him on the spot.
Seven years later,
Patrick bought the livery stable
whose land,
known as Doran Court,
stayed in our family
for 100 years.
It was there
my daddy and his three brothers
were born
during and after
the First World War.

Coming Home

World War II quit
just in time
for daddy. After
fighting its way
up the boot of Italy,
his regiment boarded
a liberty ship in Genoa
bound for Japan.
He was lying
in a hammock smoking
a Camel and feeling
doomed
when the news
crackled through
the *James Longstreet's* intercom—
the Japanese had
surrendered. His ship dropped
anchor just east
of Panama Canal
and everyone cut loose
drinking rubbing alcohol cut
with pineapple juice—
"to keep ya from
goin' blind." Eight days later,
he skipped
down the gangplank
at the Brooklyn Marine Terminal,
got paid, discharged,
and that night,
believing his luck
had finally changed,

blew $20
for a taxi ride
to Greenwich—
an extravagance my mother
never let him forget.
Right away
he moved in
with the in–laws
and became obsessed
with buying a Studebaker,
finding a job and starting
a family—though
not always
in that order.

Mianus Village

A gold coast
hung on the bank of a tinsel-
glistening river
but nobody knew that in 1946
when the VA
bought the land cheap,
bulldozed a strip through
the green woods,
built 40 matchbox houses
—750 square feet each—
and rented them
to WWII veterans
who couldn't otherwise
afford a place
in the sun.
Daddy qualified
when he got laid-off
at the nail factory
and we arrived
at this launching pad
of our lives
when I turned two.
That spring mother planted
a bed of purple iris—
whose iridescent petals
brightened our days
and the kitchen table
every summer
of my boyhood.
Within a week,
Daddy cut a gate
in the chain link fence

with pointy tips,
built by the government
to save us
from drowning ourselves.
Nobody died
but Jeffrey Bell
once got seven stitches
in his throat
after bayoneting himself
on a razor-sharp prong—
a foolish
thing for sure
because two black labs
had already dug
a trench beneath
the lower rail
deep enough
for a teenybopper
to do the limbo.

Thinking Way Back

I can't remember
a damn thing
about my first three years
but at four,
I see myself
in tears sitting
on the living room rug
pulling *Bazooka* bubble gum
out of my hair
during a live broadcast
of Eisenhower's 1ˢᵗ inaugural address.
Mother sits beside me,
smoking a Chesterfield,
saying in her stern voice,
"Stop crying
and pay attention
because this is history."
The snowy picture
on our tiny *RCA Victor* TV
jumped every time a car
with worn spark plugs
drove by, but we
still sat there
in a zombie-like trance.
Ike, as mother called him,
was bald and serious
and talked long enough
for me to eat a box
of animal crackers
and fall asleep.
Later that year
mother began reading

children's classics
at bedtime
and even today
whenever I see a copy
of *Heidi* or *Treasure Island,*
I smell cigarette smoke
and looking up
see a woman with
big hazel eyes
and tiny cracks
in her ruby red
lipstick.

War Brides

Toward the back
of the village,
six wives
lived like sisters
in the springtime
of their lives,
sharing groceries,
Patti Page records
and occasional heartaches.
I can still hear them
reading Dr. Spock aloud,
fretting about polio,
and laughing at Lucille Ball.
In the early 50s,
they stayed home
raising babies,
gathering weekly
for coffee and
their favorite morning show—
Arthur Godfrey Time.
I was shy as a boy
and stuttered
so I liked to sit
quiet as a cat,
my eyes and ears—antennas
of surprise and wonder—
uploading everyday talk
and stories of the big war,
which still brought laughter
and tears to people's faces.
This one morning
I watched them

squeeze their butts
onto our swayback couch
in front of the TV set,
fanning themselves
with *Life* magazines
when that Italian heartthrob,
Julius LaRosa,
sang his number one hit,
"Eh Compari."
When they left, I went
from saucer to saucer
sipping dripped coffee
then sat on the front step,
my heart buzzing
like a bee in a bottle.
Back then,
the world beyond the village
was vague as fog,
that is until the harsh realities
of life showed up.
First, Laura Barnet
died young
of cancer, then Molly Plant
ran away with an
old boyfriend, and one by one,
mother's other girlfriends
began moving
to bigger houses
in better neighborhoods.
She never connected
with the second wave of families
moving into the village
and as the years passed
some people thought her

stuck up. All I saw
was this lioness' hunger
for her cubs,
not wanting us
to end up poor
like her and daddy,
wearing Thrift Store clothes,
driving beaters,
and whittling our bones away
working for people
with blue blood
in their veins.

Poison Ivy

In late summer,
the sunny slope
above the river
turned into a prickly oasis
of fat, spongy blackberries.
We'd gobble them down
until our bellies ached
and come home with permanent purple
stains on our T-shirts.
Stevie Roy, who at four
was no bigger than a monkey,
and I were deep in the patch
one August day
when he said he had to pee
so we both
dropped our faded dungarees
and emptied our bladders.
Two days later
Carlene Roy called mother,
who gasped once
and dragged me
as fast as my tinker-toy legs
would skip and run
down the street
to the Roy house.
There Stevie
sat naked in the kitchen sink,
staring at us
with brown animal eyes
while Annie Wolfe,
a registered nurse
and the unofficial village doctor,

trickled water and baking soda
on his private parts.
Right away
Mrs. Roy,
whose flowery perfume
and red-bowed bouffant
already spiked in me
dangerous levels of testosterone,
asked in her soft Southern drawl
if I knew what happened
to little boys
who didn't go home
to use the bathroom.
I had no idea
what she was talking about
until she took her son
by the hand
and cried, "You must
see to believe!"
Stevie rose
in the sun-drenched window
like ET,
his red swollen scrotum
bigger
than a birthday balloon.
Even mother,
who had once changed
bandages
at the soldiers'
convalescent home,
turned aside
at the peculiar aberration.
With dead-eyed shame,
Stevie splashed down

and Annie drizzled
more of her concoction
on a poison ivy rash
that had made the poor boy
scratch himself rawer
than the back side
of a mangy dog.

Safe at Home

I hated kindergarten
when I was five years old,
knowing Johnny Del Greco,
a pudgy kid with potato chip ears
and an Elvis sneer,
was lurking in the restroom
to bloody
my nose
and that come recess
that weaselly brown-noser
Jimmy McGuire
would turn my body
into a punching bag
when no teachers were looking.
One February morning,
I slipped out of bed
without waking my brother
and tiptoed across
the creaky floorboards
to mother's bedroom
where I hesitated
until I saw the orange glow
of a cigarette.
Without a word,
I ran to the warm-hearted home
of mother's dreams
and laid my head
on the billowy softness
of her pillow.
She pulled the covers
around my neck and pretty soon
a warm feeling

calmed my mind.
Every once in a while
she'd take a drag
and blow smoke
towards the ceiling. Slowly
the morning lights
lit the floral wallpaper,
giving shape
to the mahogany dresser,
the vanity with the cracked mirror,
and the 1941 picture of
daddy in a rented suit
and mother
in her wedding dress
at the Pickwick Arms Hotel—
four months before
he got drafted
and disappeared
somewhere in Europe
for "the duration."
When a beam of light
touched my face, I snapped
my eyes shut
and pulled the sheet above my ears.
Mother stuffed out
the cigarette and
began running
her fingers
through my wiry hair.
Their soothing touch,
present to this day,
made my eyelids heavy
but I can still hear
her whispering,

"Don't worry puppy,
you're safe
with me."

Halloween

One year
Howie Shiner,
draped in torn bed sheets
and blowing
smoke rings
from a Marlboro cigarette,
led us kids
around the village
for trick or treating.
But first, he gathered us
in a circle
for bulb-popping snapshots
and a ghost story.
Dressed in homemade costumes
and sweaty plastic masks,
expressive no doubt
of our embryonic personalities,
we were cap-gun-toting cowboys,
painted Indians, witches,
pirates (my dream occupation),
and fairy princesses.
I was swaying
back and forth
as Howie asked
if we knew the real meaning
of Halloween.
When we shook our heads no,
he whispered,
"It is the one night
of the year
when the living dead
walk the earth."

Deep in the woods,
wind rustled through the trees
and an owl hooted
as we edged close
to one another.
Howie raised his hand
and warned us to stay close
because goblins
always grabbed stragglers.
I squeezed Indian maiden
Barbara Greene's hand,
glad to know
she was two years older
and packing a real tomahawk.
Just then dry leaves crackled
in the underbrush
and out came
a black-cloaked devil:
pitchfork, tail, red horns and all—
a specter that did more
to make us good Christians
than all the church sermons
of our young lives. We grabbed
one another in terror
screaming "Nooo!" as
Doug Sadowski,
a man who mother said
was already showing
signs of madness,
removed his satanic mask
and laughed hysterically
to the delight of 20 back-slapping
hooting parents.
Howie the ghost

took one last drag,
twitched his ciggie
into the grass,
and marched us
down the street
to get the candy.
One person not happy
was mother who
later spoke low
to daddy, saying
it was no wonder
Jackie was afraid
of the dark.

7 Years Old and Doomed

I remember sitting
at the kitchen table,
smelling chicken wings
in the frying pan
and staring at my broken arm,
ten minutes after falling off
Mr. Morano's stonewall.
My little arm
looked like a bridge
that had collapsed
at midstream, fingers trembling
like the petals
of the purple iris
in the vase beside me. Mother
kept saying, "Saints Save Us,"
as she dialed Annie Wolfe.
I bit my lip until it bled,
sure I was ruined—
a one-armed bag of woe,
a beggar on the sidewalk
of life rattling a cup
for small change.
Pretty soon
Annie, breathing hard,
appeared with a bang of the door.
I stared at the black curls
on her moist forehead.
as she wrapped
my arm in a cotton bunting
and tied it off with blue ribbons
after diagnosing
two clean breaks

with no danger
of compounding.
She patted my head
and said I would be fine—
as long as there were
no complications.
Right away my brother Dennis,
grinning slyly,
tapped mother's arm
and asked if that meant
he'd get the bedroom
to himself
if there were
complications.

Tires

The Butler house
at the end of the street
reeked of gasoline fumes
which I loved to inhale
whenever their boy Buddy
and I went inside for *Kool-Aid*
and slices of *Wonder Bread*—
you know the kind,
guaranteed to "build strong bodies
12 ways" especially
when splattered
with butter and sugar.
Buddy's father was a truck driver
with an Elvis pompadour
who always wore
a turquoise work shirt
with *Floyd* stenciled
above his breast pocket.
His wife, Betty Lou,
was a big-breasted woman
with a green and a blue eye
who held Floyd's hand
in public and wasn't shy
about French kissing him
when he came off the road.
I loved the way the Butlers
turned a wrecked '53 Chevy
into a playhouse,
lined their driveway
with white-wall retreads,
made wind chimes out of hubcaps,
and filled a backhoe tire

with sugary sand
direct from Daytona Beach.
Best of all was
a tire swing
dangling from a long rope
on a knotty oak limb.
I can still feel the queasy rush
as the tire
soared like a black vulture
over the shimmering river.
Betty Lou
liked me a lot
and always asked
me when Jackie was gonna
get a girlfriend,
which made me nervous
because I never knew
which eye to look at
when talking to her.

Lockjaw

This Friday night, daddy
and his brothers
were standing in the kitchen
drinking Rheingold
and I was in the living room
partially listening to them,
partially watching *Topper*,
my favorite show—
you know the one
starring the Kirbys
and Neil, their alcoholic dog
(all three ghosts)
who haunt this banker,
Cosmo Topper,
the only human permitted to see them—
and partially playing
with this rusty pocket knife,
just found in the Mianus River.
On TV, George Kirby
slid an empty gin bottle
into the cupboard as
the Toppers walked
into the kitchen
to fix martinis. Finding
the bottle empty, Mrs. Topper
asked her husband,
"Cosmo, dear,
have you been nipping again?"
Topper looked down to see
this phantom St. Bernard slurping
his booze, which made me laugh
aloud and slip off

our green Naugahyde hassock.
Sure enough, the knife
cut my finger
and blood began squirting.
I ran to the bathroom
and doctored it up
with mercurochrome
and a wad of Kleenex.
No sooner had I returned
than Uncle Dipper asked,
"Can you believe
what happened
to Marty Keen's mother?"
To which daddy replied,
"It was a damn shame
for her to live 77 years
and die of lockjaw."
The fatal disease
had set in after
the old woman stepped on
a rusty nail.
Almost unconsciously,
I began working my jaw
on its hinges
as Uncle Louie said,
"The widow had tried to call
for help at the end
but her jaws
were locked tighter
than a liquor store
on Sunday."
Just then
my molars began aching
so I started rolling my jaw

in slow easy circles
to keep it from locking up
on me.
I kept up this therapy
for two fearful weeks
but never told anyone
until now.

Why Gunner Drank Warm Beer

Daddy said Gunner
was a natural born killer
but I didn't know
what that meant
until one Saturday
about dusk
when his daughter Lisa
screamed, "Snake"
and we all ran to
her backyard
to see a Copperhead
slithering across
the gray bark
of an oak tree.
Pretty soon
half the kids in the village
were staring at its bronze bands
and flickering tongue.
Right away
Gunner pushed us aside,
took one look
at the snake
and decapitated it
with a hatchet,
then aimed
his bloodshot eyes at us
and belched, "Now git
the hell outta here—
all of ya."
Later that night
Gunner showed up
with a rattling case

of warm Schaefer beer
that daddy said tasted
like horse piss,
but kept swigging anyway
because he loved
to get Gunner talking
about machine-gunning Nazis
from Normandy to Nuremberg.
By 10 o'clock
I was in bed
crooking my neck
for another story
when I heard
Gunner crying like a baby
and mother whispering to him.
Sobbing between words,
he moaned,
"Sonofabitch, Mary,
I'm so goddamn scared
agoin' to hell,
it's killin' me"
to which she replied,
"Just because you been
to the devil's gate,
Joseph,
don't mean
you gotta go in."

Trucks

Twice a week,
white panel trucks
delivered milk
and bread
to our doorsteps.
Late afternoon,
our ears always perked up
at the sound of bells.
We would run home
for nickels and dimes
then line up single file
for orange, grape and
root-beer popsicles
handed out by Uncle Bill,
the Tiptop Ice Cream man.
Once a week at dusk
a Woody station wagon
slowed to a stop and out popped
a small man
with wire–rimmed glasses,
who smiled and saluted
as Barbara Greene led us
in the rhythmic chant:
"Dan-Dan the Egg Man."
We kept our distance
from the junk man,
who had more tattoos than teeth,
and broadcast his arrival
banging a hammer
on a frying pan,
which made mother vow
she'd throw her tin cans

in the garbage
before selling
to that rude man.
Late in the summer
a mud-splattered dump truck
would roll
up the street
and a man who looked
like the wrestler Haystacks Calhoun
would lean his big buffalo head
out the window and holler
"Water-meloooooooon"
over and over again.
Mother rued
the arrival of moving vans
which meant another woman
was escaping the village,
leaving her
with one less friend
and this painful knot
in her stomach,
knowing
her moment in the sun
was passing by.

Kittens

A handful
of purring fur balls
with bony necks
was all they were
one week
after birthing
and everyone wanted
to pet those kittens
so Eleanor put them
in a cardboard box
lined with a white baby blanket
and brought them out
for a "show and tell."
Almost at once,
Max, the Butler's old mongrel,
began sniffing the air
and stuck his nose in the box.
The next thing
I knew, he
was biting and shaking the new life
out of each kitten.
Eleanor picked up
her favorite, Snowball,
still spurting blood,
and shrieked louder
than an air raid siren.
I just looked at
those bloodied kittens,
knowing I'd see
them again
that night.
The next morning,

Max lay dead
in the street
beside a broken
baseball bat.
No one knew
who did it
but I overheard
daddy say
he'd bet his paycheck
Gunner was that damn dog's
judge, jury and
executioner.

Sergeant Major

Leonard Finn was
a WWII Purple Heart
with cold eyes
and lungs full
of cigarette smoke.
Whenever home, he always sat
in an overstuffed
recliner. He had moved
his wife Aggie,
a big-hipped woman,
and two shy sons,
who never made eye contact,
into the village
when the Army
promoted him
to Recruitment NCO
at the Greenwich Post Office,
which he called
worse duty than
Pork Chop Hill
in Korea.
When in the Finn house,
I always found myself staring
at the red and green
"Bound for Glory"
tattoo on the Sergeant's forearm
and wondering why
his hands shook
so much.
Daddy and Charlie Greene
liked to visit
their old Army buddy

on Sunday nights
to watch *Victory at Sea*
and coax war stories out of him,
but he'd just shake his head,
blow gray smoke
through his nostrils
and clink the ice
in his tumbler for Aggie
to fire him up again.
Once I overheard
her tell mother
that Leonard
worried her to death
because he was always
doing dangerous things,
like standing outside
in lightning storms,
speeding on winding roads,
and walking on thin river ice
in early winter.
One New Year's Eve
parties rocked
the village
and mother and daddy
didn't come home
until after midnight.
I awoke to hushed tones,
something
about a house fire,
before falling back to sleep.
The next morning
Dennis and I looked out
the window to see
wisps of smoke escaping

from the sergeant's chair,
now dumped
in the woods
behind the Finns' house.
We were soon poking sticks
into the box springs
when Dougie Finn,
came out and stammered
that that that
his father
had fallen asleep in his chair
because the Army
worked him so hard.
The boy's eyelids were
fluttering so much
that even we knew
he was fibbing.
Only later
did I hear Mr. Greene
tell daddy that
if Aggie hadn't smelled smoke,
Lenny the Lush
would've burned down
the house
and everyone in it.

How I Cured Dante of Dares

We were playing in the woods
behind Cappy Moore's house,
which that day meant
gawking at a *Playboy* magazine
centerfold while sharing
a pinched cigarette,
taking time out
to break up dog fights,
and pepper squirrels
with BBs,
after which
I began whittling
on a twig
with daddy's Bowie knife,
which prompted Dante
to once again begin talking
about dares.
Bothered by his
never-ending provocations,
I stopped whittling
and began slapping
the knife down on a stump
like I was dicing
an onion. Dante,
who had been smoking
since nine,
put down his cigarette
and stretched
an index finger
across the stump
then double-dog dared me
to see how close

I could come,
saying, "Whadda, chicken
or something?"
Without thinking,
I dropped the blade hard
and felt the steel vibrating
in the soft pulp
where Dante's fingertip
now lay and he saw it too
and began screaming
and jumping up and down
like a chimpanzee in a cage.
I stood there,
not breathing,
staring bug-eyed
at the red dots
on the knife, knowing
I'd be sent
to reform school
for life.
Stevie spoke up first,
saying it took courage
to teach Dante a lesson,
at which point I exhaled
and went back
to whittling
until Teddy looked
at the knife
and said it was a good thing
Dante hadn't put
his head down
on that stump.

The Natural

People said Frankie Santo,
who at 13 always wore
a tight T-shirt
with a pack of cigarettes
rolled up in his sleeve,
was jailbait
because he stole shit
just for the fun of it,
carried a dagger in his belt
and sprayed graffiti on street signs.
Still everyone agreed
he was an amazing athlete,
bound for glory if
he could stay out of prison.
When I was 12, Frankie
swept up sand and broken glass
on a side street,
painted white foul lines
and set burlap bags
at just the right distances
from a real home plate,
snitched from a Little League
baseball diamond.
Once a baseball unraveled
on the tarred street,
Frankie would call time,
wrap the core
in black friction tape
and fire the new ball to the pitcher
saying, "On widda game."
One evening with streetlights
dimmed by swarms

of gray moths,
Frankie locked
his tiny black eyeballs
onto a high speed ball
and cracked it
five houses up street
where it disappeared
like a seal through
a sheet of ice,
right where Howie Shiner
had parked the windshield
of his brand new
1959 Corvair.
It was a tape measure shot
that ended the season and got
Frankie the brag
that he once hit a ball
that would have been
a home run
in Yankee Stadium.

Uncle Johnnie in the Living Room

After his wake
at Riley's Funeral Parlor,
daddy and his brothers
bribed their uncle's hearse driver
to detour through Bruce Park
to Cos Cob and across
the bridge to Mianus Village
before returning
to the church service.
As soon as the funeral procession
stopped in front of our house,
the rear door
of this black Cadillac opened
and before you could say *sacrilege*,
Uncle Johnnie's nephews
wheeled his coffin
on a rickety bier
into our living room
and unscrewed the lid
for a traditional Irish farewell.
Mother and I came through the door
with Johnnie's widow,
Aunt Veronica,
who could have stopped
the desecration
right there but Uncle Richie
whispered something
about living in the moment
and put a glass of sherry
in her hand,
at which point she agreed
it was a grand idea

to see her husband
one more time.
I hadn't gone to the wake,
because mother thought the sight
might warp my development
so he was the first corpse
I'd ever seen.
From the strained look on mother's face,
it was clear
she'd make daddy pay later.
I recall inching close
to the casket and gasping.
Uncle Johnnie's face was gray
as cement and his bow tie
was loose and crooked.
I found myself staring at
this gold pocket watch
ticking on his chest—
all the time wondering
if he'd need it
where he was going.
I kept expecting
his eyes to pop open,
give me a wink,
and climb out of that
wooden straightjacket,
as Uncle Dipper called it,
to join his nephews
in the kitchen,
where they were slamming
Jameson shots
and entertaining one another
with funny stories
about his life and times.

Before long, a minister arrived
and everyone joined him
in the *Lord's Prayer*
after which
daddy and his brothers
dropped to their knees
and commenced bawling,
their tears
falling like waterfalls,
as a pallbearer
dropped the lid
and sealed the casket
for the last time.

Sister Annunciata

Never killed anyone
but I expected
death that day
when rosary beads rattling,
she swooped down on me
just as I let fly a spitball.
Unlike most nuns
who were meek and mild
brides of Christ,
this one was a reincarnated
bride of Frankenstein
who worked her ruler
like a switchblade
and cut my knuckles
until they bled.
Bobby Wizenski,
a born wise guy,
got it bad
one Wednesday morning
during a Catechism Bee.
I said a prayer for him
when he drew the question,
"What are the Eight Beatitudes?"
He smiled at sister and said,
"They're the new family
that just moved
to Riverside Lane." Well
she was on him like Jesus
on the moneychangers,
breaking
her ruler
on his raised arms

then hitting him
with a haymaker
that would have floored
Floyd Patterson.
It wasn't funny,
of course,
but Bobby started
carrying home
his Baltimore Catechism
after that.

Bony Herring

Just below the stone dam
splitting the Mianus River
from Cos Cob harbor,
millions of bony herring
spawned every spring.
And we were there
to snag them with triple hooks
and scoop fish
out of the water
in bulging
dip nets. We never
ate herring,
hated them in fact,
but made good money
selling shiners,
as we called them,
to the black folks
who would drive up
from Harlem
for a gospel-praising,
spiritual-singing harvest.
When fish were running,
they would lose their minds,
whopping and hollering, pointing
to silvery schools beneath the water
and flashing wads of dollar bills
at us. Every time
we climbed
the slippery footpath
on the rocky hill beside
the dam's power house—
lugging bushel baskets

full of big-eyed shiners—
they welcomed us
like Rock n' Roll stars. One
Sunday morning, I saw
a tall man with chiseled cheekbones
step out of a pink Cadillac,
slide on his tailbone
to the water's edge
and wade in
with a borrowed net, scooping,
screaming, praising
God Almighty
for bony herring.
In the water, we dodged
flying hooks and
rip currents
when the tide was changing.
One bright April afternoon,
I trudged out to the middle
of the dam
in daddy's hip boots,
stepped into a hole,
lost my balance,
and suddenly felt gushing water,
heavy as a boulder,
on my shoulders.
It flipped me over
and held me under the
cascading torrent,
my eyes seeing
glimmers of a rainbow,
my mind thinking
this is how
you die . . . that is

until the tumbling water
kicked me free
and I surfaced,
trembling, coughing,
and thanking Jesus
to be alive.

Widow Donahue

I can still see
the liver spots
on her veiny hands
and this angelic translucence
in her snowy hair
that July afternoon
when I stopped mowing
her patch of grass
and came in for lemonade.
She sat in a satin rocking chair
with an open scrapbook
on her lap and the heat on high.
When I sat down,
she tapped a photograph, saying,
"This one's my husband."
You could see laughter
in the man's face
but I didn't say anything
because her eyes
were dreamy, staring at something
I could never see until now.
Her little house
was silent except for the ticking
of a grandfather clock
and a soft breeze blowing
through the honeysuckle.
I looked at the red spidery cracks
on her cheeks and wondered
what it would be like
to be old and living
alone on memories
and TV dinners.

After a few minutes,
she gazed
through dusty lace curtains
to the river and said
he still mowed the grass
at 83. I guessed
I wouldn't be pushing
a mower that long,
at which
she shook her head,
sighed and said, "Lord,
that man knew
how to live."

Why Father MacNamara
Went to Caribou

It was a lot of things,
like not wearing
his Roman collar, swearing,
telling jokes
from the altar, the way
he twirled married women
at parish dances,
but the real decider came
one New Year's morning
when Monsignor Ganley
caught the curate
in his shorts, washing
the priest-mobile and singing
"Danny Boy." The 6-pack
of Budweiser, half empty,
on the hood didn't help
matters nor did
Sister Superior's complaint
that Father Mac
had been sipping
on a quart bottle
of Ballantine ale
while listening
to the nuns' confessions.
We altar boys
were sorry to see
him go because he
was a cool priest
who didn't get unhinged
when we rang the bells
at the wrong time

or burnt holes
in the altar linen
when lighting candles.
We liked him enough
that a few of us
considered vocations—
until we got clued in
on that celibacy thing.
The new assignment
came out of the Bishop's office
ordering him to an
Indian mission
in Caribou, Maine,
practically in the Arctic Circle,
where he'd have time
to reflect
on his "divine calling."
Father Mac shrugged
it off, saying
it wouldn't be too bad
if he could find
a young squaw
to be his housekeeper
and stock up enough booze
to keep the cold out.

How Mrs. Emerson Saved the River

A half-mile up river
where drooping
willow branches canopied
water lilies
and shaded a wetland
full of bulrushes and cattails,
an old woman lived alone
in a white clapboard house.
When her husband Harry
was alive,
they had lobbied
for a sewer system
and stopped the Gorge sawmill
from spewing
gooey poison
downstream.
For 10 years now,
the old battle ax,
as daddy called her,
had been crusading
to ban motorboats
on the Mianus
because they made wakes
that flooded her bank
of blue violets
and white columbines,
disturbed the peace,
and left gasoline slicks
in a marsh where
fish eggs hatched
and tadpoles swam.
She finally got her way

when one of God's fools
shot a metal arrow
through the neck
of a trumpeter swan
after chasing it down
in a speedboat.
The swan lived
and his picture made
all the papers,
including daddy's favorite
source of truth and wisdom,
The New York Daily News.
Even he signed
Mrs. E's petition
to the Board of Selectmen,
knowing it would end his days
of throwing down
a few beers and water skiing
behind Billy Barton's
mahogany flyer,
which could break 50 mph
when the waters of the Mianus
lay flat as an ironing board.

Coach Garfolo, Me and the Truth

I peddled my bike
to Binney Park
with my baseball
glove on the handlebar
to watch the Greenwich Gas tryouts
and let Matty
persuade me
no one would ever know
I was four months too old
to play little league baseball.
The coach, a volcano of a man
who mother joked
had learned to swear before
he was weaned,
read the rules
and sent kids out
to their tryout positions.
After briefly battling my conscience,
I crossed the white line, trotted
out to second base, kicked
the dust out of the bag,
and began
scooping up grounders
and firing bullets to first base
just like the great
Jackie Robinson.
Pretty soon, Mr. Garfolo came
running out,
pulled his pants up
over his sagging belly,
and announced
I was his second baseman,

and we were going to win
the bloody-ass championship
this year. I made
three practices
before mother learned
of my lie
and called coach,
who nearly broke down
on the phone, saying, "Ahh,
Mary, you just blew
a hole in my goddamn
million dollar infield."

Serenity on a Mudflat

Just because Ike
lived alone
in a rotting wooden boat
stuck in the mud
of Cos Cob Harbor,
urinated off the stern
and sat Zen-like
for hours
on the foredeck,
people said he was crazy.
Hatchet lines carved up
his ruddy face
and he smelled of fish and sweat
but we didn't care.
He was full of stories
about dodging U-boats
on the North Atlantic run
and catching swordfish
on Georges Bank.
At 10, I loved
feeling his bait minnows
flicker through my fingers.
Ike didn't have a penny
in the bank
but always said
it was better to live
a simple life
on the water
than a desperate one
on the land.
I ran down to the dock
one foggy Saturday morning

after hearing sirens
and saw two firemen
carrying the old fisherman,
red bony arms
stretched straight out,
to shore
where they bent down his limbs
and laid the old sailor
in a black rubber bag.
Even though Ike said
death was nothing more than
the start of a new life,
for weeks
I just couldn't get the words
rigor mortis
out of my head.

Paper Boy

Ricky Holmes sold me
his *Greenwich Time* paper route
for $10, a Mickey Mantle
baseball card,
and a promise to
let him copy
my algebra homework.
On Friday afternoons,
I'd knock on 50 doors
to collect 75 cents each
for the week's deliveries.
Most people tipped
a quarter or so
but not Mr. Hines,
a retired
English teacher
who made my week,
one October day,
by inviting me
into his book-bound living room
and slipping me a $5 tip.
His latest poem
had just been published
in the *Fordham Review*.
He called it "The Subjunctive Mood"
and asked his wife to read it aloud:
If only
Adam disliked apples,
Pilate freed Jesus,
Mozart lived to 80,
Lincoln hated plays,
the Archduke survived Sarajevo,

Hitler been a pacifist,
Arabs loved Jews,
the atom bomb fizzled,
communists admired capitalists,
Oswald missed,
and for you
and me, dear,
Ponce de Leon found
the Fountain of Youth.

That Christmas, Mr. Hines gave me a
copy of Robert Frost's *Collected Poems,*
which have been whispering
in my ears ever since.

Black Birds in a White Doves' Nest

No one locked their doors
until Laura Barnet died
and her family moved out.
That's when the VA
integrated the village
with a black family.
Sailor and Esther Thomas
moved in on a wet, snowy March day.
I ran to the front door at the sound
of a backfire to see
a rusty Ford pick-up truck
with two skinny boys
wearing bib overalls and floppy woolen hats
riding on the running boards.
Right away daddy came up
behind me and pronounced, "There goes
the neighborhood." I had no idea
what that meant
but was curious to see
these new neighbors.
The family struggled
getting furniture out of the cargo bed
but no one came to their aid,
not even when Mrs. Thomas slipped
and a sopping mattress
drove her red and yellow scarfed head
into the gray slush. Mother sighed
at the scene and whispered,
"It's sad
but they'd be better off
living with their
own kind."

We kept our distance
from the two boys, Moses and Aaron,
who always pointed their eyeballs
at the street.
Even so, we often made jokes
about coloreds
behind their backs.
That all changed for me
the next Spring
when herring were running
below the Mianus dam.
I was sitting on a flat rock
in waders, waiting for the tide to drop,
when I spotted Aaron Thomas
at the water's edge
casting for shiners
with a bamboo pole tethered to a triple hook.
Pretty soon
he snagged something underwater
and commenced pulling
with all his might.
Just then the hook and line broke free
and snapped at the boy
like a cowboy's whip.
A barb ripped
into his nose
barely missing his eye.
It hit him like an ice pick
and he fell backwards.
Without thinking, I ran to his side
and asked if he was okay. He was trembling
all over and
gobs of red blood
were falling onto his dungarees.

He screwed his face up
and big tears welled in his eyes
but he didn't cry.
I didn't know what to do
other than put my hand on his shoulder
and say, "It's gonna be all right."
That's when he bent his head towards
me and I felt the warmth of his ebony cheek
on my hand. It's funny but in those few moments
everything I knew about Blacks
changed. Aaron bled
just like the rest of us; he felt pain
and anguish just like us.
Beneath my skin I was just like him.
In that instant
of shared humanity,
I knew the grownups
in Mianus Village and beyond
were dead wrong
in denying Black people
a full and free life
just because of the color
of their skin.

When Krissy Lee Stood Up

the first day of eighth grade
to answer a geography question,
I nearly swallowed a peach pit.
I always knew she had
nice legs and a pretty face
but now she had breasts—
round, high riding ones that quivered
when she sat down.
I could see the white straps
on her bra and knew
we would never catch fire flies
or play hide and seek
again. She held her
head high, not turning
or even blushing
when horny Phil Vecchio
snorted like a pig at her.
She was the kind of girl
you wanted to slow dance
with but were afraid to ask.
I'd sit there in class, drawing our initials
in Cupid hearts
as teacher, her draped upper arms
blocking half the blackboard,
droned on and on
about crops and animals
and minerals
of Ecuador, Paraguay
and God knows where else.
When we changed seats
for the new year,
I ended up beside Krissy,

all the time feeling
this pain in my stomach
cured only by a shared glance
or a fleeting smile.
Then one day I saw
a high school boy's class ring
on a chain
around her neck and
my heart skipped a beat.
All that was left
was the numb recognition
that she'd never
ever fall asleep
in my loving arms.

An Unwanted Christmas Present

On Christmas Eve
Mickey K and his team
of 14-year-old semi-pros
skated across the new
river ice
for our annual hockey game.
He called his team
the Sheephill Terminators
and us the Mianus River Rats,
but we didn't care.
We were street smart runts
without jerseys
or even shin guards.
Following the usual trash talk
about us being
a chicken-shit team,
we got a face off at dusk.
Mickey scored two
lightning-fast goals
after which Petey Merton
and I dropped back
to trip him every time
he got the puck.
Then we slapped
the black rubber disk
up ice to my brother,
a bear on skates,
who scored twice and
Mickey was mad.
He took the puck across center ice
and wound up for
his famous rocket shot.

I can still hear our goalie bellowing:
"No liftin', no liftin,' "
as Petey skated hard
for Mickey. That
was his first mistake;
not ducking
was the second.
The hockey puck
hit Petey
between the eyes,
dropping the poor boy
like a shot duck.
He got up
after a few minutes,
shaky but alive
with the game called
for attempted murder.
Later at the midnight
candlelight service,
I got a good look
at Petey's twin shiners,
which his mother
told everyone
was not the kind
of Christmas present
she had expected
from her son.

Frog Legs

One high-school summer,
Teddy and I rowed
my dinghy upriver
to Mrs. O'Connell's wetland
and poached frogs
only to get caught
and sent to juvenile court
where Judge Tynsdale Harrington III,
all chalky face and crimson lips,
presided in black robes,
ten feet above
our terrified bodies.
He looked at the charge sheet
then stared at us
with fiery eyeballs
and demanded,
"What in God's good name
were you audacious punks doing
with a burlap bag
full of frogs?"
I stood still as a flagpole
waiting for Teddy to speak,
but he just gulped and gulped,
never saying nothing.
I had no pity
on him
because we would've been
home free
except he tripped
on an untied shoelace
while running across the widow's lawn,
then got himself treed

by her German Shepherd.
Pretty soon the old woman came out,
leashed the dog
and looked into our bag
which made her wheeze,
release the beast
and call the cops.
Now two weeks and
endless lectures later
about being sent upriver
to make license plates
and suffer physical humiliation,
we stood before
the reincarnation
of Count Dracula himself.
So I confessed
we had an agreement
with Julius
at the Clam Box restaurant
to deliver fresh frogs
to him for $7 a bag
at which point everyone
began talking at once
until the judge hammered
them silent
with a gavel
loud as a sonic boom
and ordered the bailiff
to bring this Julius fellow
to his chambers
with all due haste.

Rock Thrower

Davey and I
were floating
on the Mianus
one summer day
when a rock sliced
through the water
between us.
We weren't surprised
thinking Frankie Santo
had gotten out of work early
and headed down
to the river
for a little swim
and mayhem.
We treaded water
and dodged rocks,
falling like mortars
around us
until a round crashed
on my head.
Davey pulled me ashore
or I would surely have drowned,
especially since
hot blood, streaming
through my fingers,
filled my head with
a kaleidoscope
of spinning colors.
Almost at once,
my brother
Dennis came running up,
saying it was an accident,

that he didn't mean to hit me
so I forgave him
but not so our neighbor
Donnie McHugh
who sped us to
Greenwich Hospital ER
after punching Den
hard enough in the gut
to bruise his backbone.
An hour later,
I lay on the table
grimacing as Dr. Murphy
sewed me up and made jokes
about brotherly love.

Atlantic City on $200

We packed the red station wagon
all week
for a four-day trip
because it was our first
vacation and we were excited.
Mother had visited Atlantic City
and its great boardwalk
as a child and wanted
us to see it too. Daddy
didn't care for vacations,
but he was curious
to see Luscious Lucy,
a bareback rider on a white horse
who every hour
plunged off the steel pier's high tower
into a pool of water.
We stayed at the Green Dunes Motel,
built right over a drained marsh,
which the owners said
was a shining example
of 20th century progress,
but no one had evicted
a squadron of bloodthirsty mosquitoes
who ate us alive.
After three days, mother
had $5 left which went
for lunch and tolls
on the Jersey Turnpike
where we got a flat tire
and sick to our stomachs
after breathing green fumes

billowing out of a 16-wheeler
that swerved to miss
a deer and flipped over
before our very eyes.

Gypsy

As kids
we shot marbles
in the grass and chewed
Wrigley's gum
until our jaws ached.
Eva Ruth
was the next-door girl
who I secretly loved
even though she had
greasy hair
and needed braces.
Times got hard
after her father died at 43
of lung cancer
and her mother lost
a waitressing job
at the Town House
after showing up with booze
on her breath.
The summer after our freshman year,
I remember Eva walking
down our street
in pedal pushers
and a yellow polka-dot bikini top
that mother called risky.
One sweltering Saturday afternoon
Eva came over
and said, "Let's go tubing."
I was whistling happy
as I inflated two inner tubes
for our watery date
but anticipation

proved to be the highlight
of the day.
Once on the river,
Eva just floated in silence.
A couple of times
we made eye contact
but she'd catch her breath
and shake her head no.
Back at the dock, she just said,
"I gotta get out of here"
and walked past me.
I wanted to hug her
but lacked the confidence,
courage really,
to do so.
Late that night, I heard
a screen door bang
and knew she was gone.
Eva's mother blamed
her Roma blood
for the disappearance
and every night sat in the dark
sipping Ballantine beer,
waiting, waiting
for her baby girl
to come home.

The Day the Music Died

No football practice
that Friday afternoon
in November 1963
so we grabbed our books
and tumbled out of Hampton Hall
onto Ray Dutton's bus.
The Ronettes were singing
Be My Baby
on a transistor radio
so we danced the Stroll
down the aisle
all the time chanting,
"So won't you, please
be my,
be my baby…
my one and only baby."
I sidled into a seat
next to Maureen Wolfe.
"For every kiss you give me,"
I purred in her ear,
"I'll give you three."
She shrugged me off,
lit a cigarette,
and blew smoke in my face.
Seconds later
the song's drum roll died
in mid beat
and DeeDee Vecchio
came running down the aisle
with this bewildered look
on her face.
"The President's been shot!"

was all she said.
Maureen locked eyeballs with me,
threw her cigarette
out the window
and made the sign of the cross.
Then everyone was talking,
crying and screaming.
In the back of the bus,
Tommy Thompson prophesized,
"If JFK dies,
Johnson's gonna drag us
into a stupid-ass war."
I sat there biting my lip,
praying
our silver-tongued young president
was just wounded.
The next thing I remember,
Mr. Dutton stood up,
shifted his weight a few times
and said,
"Kennedy's dead."
I still see
the President's horse-drawn
flag-draped caisson
trailed by a riderless stallion
with boots reversed
in its stirrups,
clip clopping
to Arlington Cemetery
where black-veiled Jackie Kennedy
lit an eternal flame
at JFK's gravesite
so that, as she later said,

his dream
of a just new world
would never be extinguished.

Moving On

1.

During the spring semester
of my second year at college,
I missed the move
that ended 18 years
of living in Mianus Village.
For five years
mother had saved every dollar
so she and daddy could buy
a middle-class house
with a porch and a garage,
bordered by a real garden (her dream).
I showed up in mid-May,
sat down on the new couch
with a leaky BIC pen
in my back pocket,
soaked the dining room ceiling
by not putting
the shower curtain
inside the bathtub,
and one night
took Dennis' motorcycle
out in the rain,
promptly skidded,
fell off, wrecking the bike
and my knee—
all of which convinced
the family
that perhaps a college education
was overrated.

2.

I stepped out
of an Air Force ROTC drill
to take a phone call
that the cadet commander
barked better be damned important
and there was
Aunt Peg saying
take the 6:30 PM
Mohawk flight home.
I kept staring
at my spit-shined shoes
thinking it was daddy
until she said,
"It's Mary"
and hung up.

3.

Mother was talking
on the phone
when a vessel
in her head popped
like a balloon
and she passed out. Later
Dr. Beck, her boss,
said Mary suffered
no pain
and calmly read the results
of the autopsy.
It seemed strange
to hear her talk

professionally
about someone
who wasn't just another case.
At the end of the funeral though,
I spotted the doctor
in the back pew
shaking and sobbing
like a spanked child.
I wanted to stop
and hug her but the procession
kept pushing us forward.
Light was streaming
in our faces through
a stained glass window
translucent with yellow
and purple flowers
and that's when it hit me
like a sucker punch—
there'd never be
another vase of iris
on the kitchen table
and I'd never see
my mother
smiling in the sun
again.

4.

Daddy went to the family plot
at the cemetery
every day for two years,
usually with a 6-pack
of Pabst Blue Ribbon
and Uncle Richie's dog, Gypsy,

who chased rabbits while he
sat on the base
of his grandfather's obelisk,
chugged a few beers
and talked to mother
as he had done every night
for 23 years. We thought
he was going to drink himself
to death until he ruptured
his esophagus after
a weekend binge.
They saved him
by threading
black drainage tubes
through his chest
to irrigate his infected lungs.
When he came out of surgery,
his blood pressure
was so low
the nurse couldn't
give him morphine
and even Dr. Murphy said
he'd never seen anyone
in so much pain.

5.

I thought a Vietnam tour
was a sure thing
but except for a weekend trip to LA
to see the Pacific Ocean,
I never went west
of Phoenix,
where my daughter

was born
at an Air Force hospital,
2,500 miles from home.

6.

After serving
one last year of active duty
at a New York City
recruitment center,
I moved us 300 miles north
to a new life in Vermont.
Before I knew it,
I had gotten two bad jobs,
a house, a car
and divorced.
I hadn't thought
about Mianus Village
in years
until one night
I dreamed I saw Dennis
and Eddie Morley
in the middle of the river,
rocking Bobby Gregg's
aluminum rowboat
while he swung at them
with an oar, all the time
bellowing, "No good bas-turds,
no good bas-turds"
even as he and his dog Ace,
both in orange life preservers,
slowly sank to
the boat's gunwales.
The next weekend

I drove down
to Connecticut
to walk through the village
and see
the river again.

7.

I parked on Westview Place
and looked down the hill
at Mianus Village, a place
where the march of time
had forever stopped in 1960.
Above me, a lime-green canopy
of oaks and hickories,
whose swaying branches
once seemed
so dark and scary
when running home
on winter nights, shaded the
black-trodden path.
A high breeze rummaged
through trees whose
leaves had budded
and opened 50 times
since I was last here.
Near the bottom,
I came to the gnarled tree,
its trunk still carved
with our faded initials,
where Gunner,
his face frozen in time,
had killed the snake.
For a moment

I could hear the time-warped voices
of those of us
who had come of age here
when rock 'n roll was young,
before a charismatic president
got his head shot off
and his corn-pone successor
tried to conquer Vietnam,
which cost two village kids their lives
and made the country explode
in protest, drugs and agony.
No one was home at our old house
but one of mother's flowering iris—
a ghost's gift to the present—
flickered in the sun.
Daddy's gate,
hanging by one hinge,
opened with a screech.
Down the bank
rippling river water lapped
a rowboat at a splintered dock.
Almost at once I heard
people talking
in a familiar way—
echoes from the past—
and looking up
to the narrow yard
saw a weather-beaten picnic table
that for a brief moment
was covered
by a paper tablecloth
and there came a man
with thinning black hair
carrying a sirloin steak

on a paper plate
to a slim woman
with red lipstick
and two small boys
in torn dungarees
and high-top sneakers
who sat waiting
for him.

EPILOGUE

Tod's Point

In that tender time
between sheet and sleep,
wrapped in sacred darkness,
I *still* see my mother,
young and happy
in a summer dress,
facing her smiling sister.
They're spreading
a red checkered tablecloth
on a picnic table
at a grassy meadow
overlooking the long sandy beach.
Up the coastline
stands a red and white lighthouse,
even then a subliminal symbol
of hope, refuge, and strength.
High tide, the wind light,
a gray haze has cleared
and the water
is smooth as glass.
We have just come from
a swimming lesson. Today
they were teaching me
to do the doggie paddle
and float on my back.
Widowed Aunt Veronica
gives me a hand squeeze
while humming
that haunting lost love song,

The Tennessee Waltz.
Daddy and Uncle Bud drink beer
in the shade of a tulip tree,
boastful about another
subway series between
the Yankees and the Dodgers
whom daddy hates
because "dem bums"
will choke like last year.
He reaches
into the icy water
of the Scotch Cooler
for a bottle of Rheingold.
Even then I pray
it's empty. Mother
serves me a grilled hot dog,
her eyes shining
in the sunshine. Today at least
no rain clouds
or arguments
will darken the waters.
Without a care
in the world,
I dangle my legs
under the picnic table,
remembering
this one day
over and over
and over again.

ABOUT THE AUTHOR

Jack T. Scully is a longtime writer of fiction, non-fiction, and professional papers. He has penned numerous poems and stories, the blog *Pilgrim's Rest*, and currently, with J. Chris Davala, the website and Facebook page *Beyond Gridlock and Greed*. Following service in the U.S. Air Force, he worked at a number of newspapers before entering the high-tech industry. He eventually co-founded a successful high-tech company, which pioneered enabling technology for new medical procedures. Now semi-retired, he lives with his family in Vermont. This book of poems found its genesis and inspiration in the author's boyhood home in Riverside, CT, where he came of age in a VA Housing Project for returning GIs in the years following World War II.

This book is set in Garamond Premier Pro, which had its genesis in 1988 when type-designer Robert Slimbach visited the Plantin-Moretus Museum in Antwerp, Belgium, to study its collection of Claude Garamond's metal punches and typefaces. During the fifteen hundreds, Garamond – a Parisian punch-cutter – produced a refined array of book types that combined an unprecedented degree of balance and elegance, for centuries standing as the pinnacle of beauty and practicality in type-founding. Slimbach has created a new interpretation based on Garamond's designs and on compatible italics cut by Robert Granjon, Garamond's contemporary.

Copies of this book can be ordered
from all bookstores including Amazon
and directly from the author,
Jack T. Scully
PO Box 470
Colchester, VT 05446.
Please send $18 per book
plus $4.00 shipping in VT
and $6.00 beyond VT
by check payable to
Jack T. Scully.

•

For more information on the work of Jack T. Scully,
visit www.antrimhousebooks.com/authors.html.

Lightning Source UK Ltd.
Milton Keynes UK
UKHW010640060721
386714UK00001B/206